LAW OF ATTRACTION TURBOCHARGE

by Paul Piotrowski

LAW OF ATTRACTION TURBOCHARGE

~

Dedicated to my wife Drea

for always believing in me.

~

TABLE OF CONTENTS

INTRODUCTION

I have been fascinated with The Law of Attraction for almost a decade.

My research into The Law of Attraction has led me to read numerous books, watch various videos and study, interview and converse with some of the most successful Law of Attraction practitioners in the world.

Even though there is now a tremendous amount of information available on The Law of Attraction, the majority of the content of this book come from my own personal experimentation with The Law of Attraction in my life.

I see The Law of Attraction as a vehicle which can take you from where you are now, to where you want to be, if you learn how to properly operate this vehicle. In this book I will often use the analogy of using The Law of Attraction as a vehicle to get you from point A to point B, just like you would use a car.

You don't need to understand every single inner working of a car in order to be able turn it on and drive it. Similarly, although the exact way in which The Law of Attraction operates in our Universe may be a mystery to us, we don't need to understand how it works - we just need to understand how to make it work for us.

The nine strategies I will share with you in this book are not only going to help you to learn how to use The Law of Attraction as a vehicle which will take you towards the things you desire in your life, but they will also help you to turbocharge the speed at which you see results.

Enjoy the ride!

Your friend,

Paul Piotrowski

CHAPTER 1 - LAW OF ATTRACTION

Deep down in your heart, you probably already know this, but perhaps your lack of consistent success with it has left you jaded and doubtful of the fact that the Law of Attraction is real, does work, and does affect every part of your life.

As you absorb and begin to apply the information I will share with you in this book, we will not only erase any doubts you may have about the Law of Attraction, but also learn how to turbocharge your Law of Attraction results. You will begin to really believe and consciously apply the Law of Attraction in your daily life to attract the life of your dreams.

To begin with, we must first clearly define what the Law of Attraction really is.

What Is The Law of Attraction?

One of the clearest, and what I believe to be the best definitions of the Law of Attraction was written by a man who has been dead for well over a hundred years. In his book "*The Science of Getting Rich*", Wallace Wattles defines the Law of Attraction as follows:

"THERE IS A THINKING STUFF FROM WHICH ALL THINGS ARE MADE, and which, in its original state, permeates, penetrates, and fills the interspaces of the universe. A thought in this substance produces the thing that is imaged by the thought.

A person can form things in his thought, and by impressing his thought upon formless substance can cause the thing he thinks about to be created.

In order to do this, a person must pass from the competitive to the creative mind. Otherwise he cannot be in harmony with formless intelligence, which is always creative and never competitive in spirit.

A person may come into full harmony with the formless substance by entertaining a lively and sincere gratitude for the blessings it bestows upon him. Gratitude unifies the mind of man with the intelligence of substance, so that man's thoughts are received by the formless. A person can remain upon the creative plane only by uniting himself with the formless intelligence through a deep and continuous feeling of gratitude.

A person must form a clear and definite mental image of the things he wishes to have, to do, or to become, and he must hold this mental image in his thoughts, while being deeply grateful to the supreme that all his desires are granted to him.

The person who wishes to get rich must spend his leisure hours in contemplating his vision, and in earnest thanksgiving that the reality is being given to him. Too much stress cannot be laid on the importance of frequent contemplation of the mental image, coupled with unwavering faith and devout gratitude. This is the process by which the impression is given to the formless and the creative forces set in motion.

The creative energy works through the established channels of natural growth, and of the industrial and social order. All that is included in his mental image will surely be brought to the person who follows the instructions given above, and whose faith does not waver. What he wants will come to him through the ways of established trade and commerce.

In order to receive his own when it is ready to come to him, a person must be in action in a way that causes him to more than fill his present place. He must keep in mind the purpose to get rich through realization of his mental image. And he must do, every day, all that can be done that day, taking care to do each act in a successful manner. He must give to every person a use value in excess of the cash value he receives, so that each transaction makes for more life, and he must hold the advancing thought so that the impression of increase will be communicated to all with whom he comes into contact.

The men and women who practice the foregoing instructions will certainly get rich, and the riches they receive will be in exact proportion to the definiteness of their vision, the fixity of their purpose, the steadiness of their faith, and the depth of their gratitude."

~Wallace D. Wattles, "The Science of Getting Rich"

These timeless words written by Wallace Wattles were the first clear definition of the Law of Attraction which I was exposed to about a decade ago. Since then, I have read and seen dozens of movies and books on the topic of the Law of Attraction, but I have found none of them to be as clear and concise about the definition of the Law of Attraction as Wallace Wattles is in the words he wrote.

A careful study of his summary on the science of getting rich shines a bright light on what the Law of Attraction really is and what it requires of us to be able to consciously use it to attract and manifest the lives of our dreams.

Defining The Universe

In his opening statement, Wallace Wattles states that *"there is a thinking stuff of which all things are made"*. He then further states that this thinking stuff *"in its original state, permeates, penetrates, and fills the interspaces of the universe."*

What Wattles is saying is that the universe we live in is made up of an intelligent energy of sorts, which encompasses and permeates every single part our entire universe. This intelligent energy responds to and reacts, in a predictable fashion, to our energy through what we refer to as The Law of Attraction.

From this we may further deduce that since all things are made of this intelligent energy, we too must be made from it. Therefore, when this intelligent energy responds to our energy, it is really just responding to a part of itself - since obviously we are a part of it as well.

I have heard many different analogies related to this concept. One of which is that we are like a droplet of water in a vast ocean. Even though we are this droplet inside the ocean, we are also part of the ocean.

Another analogy sometimes used is that as human beings we are a small piece of consciousness, self-aware within a larger all-encompassing mass consciousness which makes up the entire universe.

Yet another way some of us choose to understand this concept is through a more religious point of view which is that we are all part of God (by whichever name you call him/her), and that God is a part of all of us.

Regardless of which label you choose to give to this *"thinking stuff"* (as Wallace Wattles calls it), for the purposes of this book I will refer to it as The Universe just so that we have a clear distinction as to what I am referring to.

If you prefer to think in religious terms, simply replace the words "The Universe" with God / Allah / Buddha / Higher Power or whichever name you call him/her. I will simply use the word "The Universe" because it is a more neutral label which I think anyone can relate to regardless of their spiritual beliefs. Even if you don't believe in any form of Higher Power, you may simply think of "The Universe" as literally all of the energy and matter in the cosmos, or as consciousness, or even as a substitute for the word "humanity".

Do not get stuck on labels, as it will just impede your success with learning how to consciously and effectively use the Law of Attraction in your life. Instead just translate the words "The Universe" to whichever label you feel most comfortable with.

The Universe and The Law of Attraction

Now that we understand what I am referring to when I use the words "The Universe", throughout this book we will explore how you can align yourself with The Universe to manifest the life of your dreams through the proper use of The Law of Attraction.

The Law of Attraction is a force in our lives which is always at work. Contrary to what some people believe, the Law of Attraction doesn't require you to believe in it or even to be aware of it, in order for it to work in your life.

The Law of Attraction is a similar force to gravity. You don't have to be consciously aware that gravity exists or even what gravity is, for it to work in your life. From the moment we are born, gravity is a part of our life even if we don't become consciously aware of it until we learn all about it in elementary school or before.

Sometimes, such as for example when we look up in the sky and see an airplane flying by, objects appear to be defying the laws of gravity. However, the same gravity which keeps us from falling off the face of the earth into outer space is just as much at work on that flying airplane as it is on ourselves.

When the Wright Brothers invented the first successful airplane, they didn't defy the rules of gravity when they achieved flight, just as birds don't defy gravity when they fly. It is only an illusion that airplanes and birds defy gravity.

In the same way, The Law of Attraction is always at work in our lives. Even when it appears as if we or someone else is defying The Law of Attraction, it is just an illusion based on our lack of understanding.

Therefore, the intention of this book is not to somehow make The Law of Attraction work better in your life as that would be impossible. The Law of Attraction is already working just as well in your life as it is in everyone else's.

The intention of this book is to help you better understand how to consciously use The Law of Attraction to manifest the life of your dreams.

In the decade or so in which I've been consciously using The Law of Attraction in my life, I have learned two important things about The Law of Attraction:

1. There are things which we can think / do / believe, which align us more with and improve our ability to consciously use The Law of Attraction in our lives and which "turbocharge" the speed in which we see tangible results.

2. There are things which we can think / do / believe, which put us out of alignment with and diminish our ability to consciously

use The Law of Attraction in our lives and which prevent us from seeing any tangible results.

In this book we will explore nine key strategies which I have found to put me in alignment with The Law of Attraction, and which help me to avoid putting myself out of alignment with it.

Both are necessary.

If we simply just focus on the things that align us with The Law of Attraction, while at the same time still doing the things which also at the same time put us out of alignment with The Law of Attraction, the results we see in our lives will be sporadic at best.

When we think / do / believe the things which align us with The Law of Attraction it is just like pressing the gas pedal in a car. When we think / do / believe the things which misalign us with The Law of Attraction, it is just like pressing the brake pedal in a car.

For a lot of us, we are simultaneously slamming down on both the gas and the brake and overheating our engines, but really not going anywhere.

Some of the strategies I will cover with you are intended to help you take the foot off the break (metaphorically speaking) and some are intended to help you put your foot on the gas pedal. By doing both, you will be able to turbocharge the speed in which you see results with consciously using The Law of Attraction in your life.

And with that, let's jump right into the very first of the nine strategies...

CHAPTER 2 - HACKING REALITY

Let's dive right into what I believe to be one of the biggest ways in which we put ourselves out of alignment with The Law of Attraction. If there is one way in which we can really take our foot off the brake, it's by applying what I will teach in this chapter.

When I was 13 years old, back in the late 1980's, I got a Tandy Color Computer for Christmas. This was one of those old style computers which you hook up to your TV, long before everyone had a computer in their home and long before the Internet as we know it today even existed.

In those days, one of my favorite things to do as a kid was to go to the store and to buy Rainbow Magazine, which was a magazine dedicated to that specific type of computer. Each month, the magazine published the source code (computer code) to a game I could play on the computer.

Essentially how it worked was that you took the code printed in the magazine and you re-typed it into the computer. This process took hours, sometimes even days to complete since at that time I was still typing with two fingers. At the end of this tedious but exciting time of re-typing every line of computer code printed in the magazine I got to run the program and was rewarded with a new video game I could play.

Of course these games were very basic compared to what we see in today's video gaming world, but at that time in the early days of video games it was a lot of fun. I would play the games for weeks and tried to finish the game before the end of the month so that I would be ready for next month's magazine with a fresh new video game to play.

At first I really enjoyed playing these games, but at one point I was playing this one game in which I found myself always dying. After hours of frustration in not being able to make it to the next level, I had an idea.

What if I could go into the programming code itself and look around to see where in the code the authors of this magazine established the amount of lives you started the game with. Since the game started with three lives, I looked for the place in the code where this was defined.

It didn't take me very long to find this and I decided to change that number to nine hundred and ninety nine lives to see what would happen. As anticipated, I now started the game off with 999 lives. I felt excited, and slightly guilty at the same time. I had programmed my first "cheat" code into a video game.

At first this was a lot of fun, because now I could actually make it past the first few levels and I got to explore all the further levels in the game before the next month's edition of the magazine came out. After a while though, I found that my game play started to get really sloppy. I really didn't care if I died anymore since I had virtually become "immortal" in the video game.

It was then that I realized that even with virtually unlimited lives, some of the levels were still difficult to get past because each time I died the game would send me back to the beginning of the level. So, I did what any 13 year old kid with the new found power to hack the very reality of his video games would do - I went looking for another way to cheat!

After a bit of studying the code, I realized that I could add in a little piece of programming code which would allow me to skip levels! If at any point in the game I got bored with a level, I could skip to the next level with the click of a button.

This was so exciting to me. I felt like a real hacker. So I launched my game, armed with 999 lives and my magic level skipping button. After playing the first level for a while, I got bored with it and skipped to level two. I played level two for a while and then skipped to level three. I got bored of level three even faster than level two so I skipped to level four, then five, then six and so on until I finished the game.

That's when I realized something very important.

All of a sudden I found myself feeling extremely depressed. Why? Because I got bored of the game so quickly, since there was no longer any challenge to it and I finished all the levels in less than an hour and now I was without a game to play for an entire month until the next edition of Rainbow Magazine came out.

It was at this time that I learned one of my first lessons related to The Law of Attraction, even though I didn't know it at the time.

What I learned is that even though we may think that we would be so happy if life only brought us every single desire without any challenge or delay, that is not true. Deep down, we all have a deeply rooted desire for things to unfold in our lives in their own perfect time, with enough challenge to help us grow and expand.

As we have all heard before, it is the journey that is important and not the destination.

So what does this mean for us in terms of aligning ourselves with The Law of Attraction?

A Hierarchy of Desires

The Universe is always responding to all of our desires through the Law of Attraction. However, it doesn't respond to all desires equally. There is a hierarchy to our conscious and unconscious desires and the Law of Attraction follows that hierarchy. Our deepest desires carry infinitely more "weight" with the Law of Attraction than any "weak" desires we create.

Our deepest desires literally shape the very fabric of our reality, even if we are not aware of them. Most of us have probably never thought about this consciously, but one of our deepest desires is the desire to live within this reality we have created for ourselves here on earth.

We don't have to consciously think about this desire for it to exist in our subconscious any more than we have to think about our desire to keep our heart beating. It's just something that happens automatically.

This deep rooted desire is at the core of everything we experience in life and it overrides almost every other desire we could have. We all have a lot of energy invested in this "earthly" reality which we live in, and it is very important for us to maintain that reality - even though I realize that consciously we probably never think about this.

So what many of us try to do as soon as we learn about The Law of Attraction is that we try to use it to hack our own reality!

Many people who first learn about the concept of The Law of Attraction think to themselves *"Ok, if this so called Law of Attraction is real, then let's see if I can manifest a Ferrari® in my driveway..."* or *"If the Law of Attraction really works, let's see if I can make money appear in front of me right now."*

In fact, many skeptics of The Law of Attraction will often present such statements as "proof" that The Law of Attraction doesn't exist. You'll hear them saying *"If The Law of Attraction really works, then let's see you make a Ferrari® appear in my driveway right now"* not realizing that if such a thing happened it would completely shatter the very fabric of their reality.

We have to realize and accept the fact that we don't want to "break reality" the way I was breaking the reality of the video games I was playing. By making myself "immortal" in the game and giving myself the ability to "skip levels" I ruined the whole experience of the video games.

Let me put it another way. What is the fastest way to get a black belt in Karate? It's very simple, you just drive out to the martial arts supply store and buy one. You don't even have to attend a single Karate class.

That isn't what we want though, is it? It's not the black belt we wrap around our waist that we want, it's the experience/abilities we learn along the journey towards becoming and earning our black belt, right?

When you try to consciously use The Law of Attraction to attract the things that you most desire in life, stop trying to attract things which would completely destroy your entire reality.

If you are currently making $2,000/m and living paycheck to paycheck, don't try to use the Law of Attraction to attract a Trillion Dollars out of thin air. If that happened it would ruin your life. Go for something that will provide you with the financial abundance you seek, but that won't ruin your entire experience of life.

Try using The Law of Attraction to attract things that you believe to be at least possible in life. If you do desire to be the world's first trillionaire I am not here to tell you that is impossible. I'm just here to tell you that you may be more successful in first attracting becoming a ten-thousandaire, and then a hundred-thousandaire, and then a millionaire and then a billionaire and then a trillionaire.

Even in these examples we are still talking about things that are possible. It probably wouldn't completely shatter your life if you became a millionaire overnight. Many people win the lottery and become instant millionaires. Their lives aren't necessarily improved by such an event, but it is possible.

However, what many of us try to do when we first learn about The Law of Attraction is that we genuinely try to manifest some kind of event that would completely shatter the world, such as making Ferrari®'s or bags of money appear out of thin air, or making the sun disappear (and no I'm not talking about an eclipse or night time). Stop doing that to yourself. Stop trying to use The Law of Attraction to try to manifest something you don't want anyways.

Deep down one of our primal desires as human beings is to maintain this reality we live in, so stop trying to hack it by using The Law of Attraction. It won't work. The Law of Attraction sees your primary desire to "maintain reality" as a much higher priority than any of your desires to "hack reality".

So if you want to become a millionaire, try attracting a "realistic" way of becoming a millionaire.

Do not try to test The Law of Attraction by trying to attract something you believe to be impossible with it. The Universe will not allow that. The Universe knows that deep down what you desire most as a human being is to maintain this reality so it will not let your desire for a Ferrari® override that primal desire we all have.

Achieving Incredible Things

Some of you may be thinking that what I am advocating is being "realistic". I am not really saying that the only thing that The Law of Attraction will manifest in your life are things that are "realistic". There are many incredible things I have manifested in my life which went far beyond what any "realist" would say is "realistic".

However, nothing I have ever manifested could be considered "impossible". For example, I have manifested things like money and free cars in my life but they all came to me in very "realistic" ways. There was always a "reasonable" explanation for everything that happened.

Even if the explanation is very improbable, The Universe always gives us what we want nicely packaged with an explanation of how it happened so that we don't end up breaking our reality and the reality of those around us.

Anything we can conceive and believe, we can achieve. But it will always come to us only after we believe it to be possible and in ways which are believable themselves.

When I have used The Law of Attraction to manifest more money in my life for example, that money always came as a result of a sudden increase in the value of my real estate investments, or a sudden rise in the value of my stock options, or a sudden inflow of new customers for my business, or other ways which are perfectly explainable within the normal rules of how reality works. Not once did The Universe make a satchel of cash appear out of nowhere in front of my eyes. If that were to happen, it would have ruined my life.

This is the first strategy to using the Law of Attraction. **Stop trying to hack reality!**

CHAPTER 3 - SPEED BUMPS AND BRICK WALLS

The Universe can help you manifest anything you have a true desire for. If the Universe can help us though, why does it seem like sometimes it's ignoring our calls?

Why is it that sometimes we ask for the simplest things from The Universe and then feel disappointed when it doesn't deliver, while other times The Universe brings us the most incredible things in life with simplicity and ease?

Why does this happen? Is The Universe some cruel jokester that likes to toy with us?

No. As you'll soon discover, we are toying with ourselves.

The shortest distance between two points is a straight line. If we want to get from Point A (where we are now) to Point B (where we want to be), the shortest path is a straight line between the two points.

But The Universe doesn't always take us from Point A to Point B in a straight line. In fact, it almost never does. Why?

To understand why the shortest path between point A and point B in our lives isn't always a straight line we have to first understand that The Universe is always working within the limitations of our beliefs. Meaning, let's say that the straight line path towards getting a bank loan from XYZ Bank is for you to go into the bank, apply for a bank loan and get it.

Well, that may be a simple solution and for a lot of people The Universe can and will provide such a simple solution, but what if you are living your life with the following limiting beliefs:

"I hate XYZ Bank. They are totally unreasonable and they only care about ultra rich people."

"XYZ Bank is very strict on lending out money. They have always rejected me."

"Nobody I know has ever gotten approved by XYZ Bank."

"XYZ Bank charges very expensive rates."

"XYZ Bank closes early every day at 4pm."

"I don't want to be with a bank that closes early."

"Banks that close early don't care about their clients."

"I once bounced a check with XYZ Bank, and they probably have it on file."

"If you bounce a check with a bank, they'll never give you a loan."

etc.

Do you see how beliefs such as these can affect The Universe's ability to help you? The Universe is always trying to help you get what you desire in the simplest, easiest and most efficient way possible, BUT it is restricted to work within the confines of <u>your</u> beliefs.

Beliefs are just thoughts which you keep thinking to yourself over and over again until you believe that they are true. Your beliefs define what is and what is not possible in your version of reality.

Beliefs work both ways. A belief such as *"Getting a loan from a bank is super easy"* can help you get a loan in an easy way, while a belief such as *"Getting a loan from a bank is difficult"* will slow things down.

Once again, beliefs are just thoughts which we say to ourselves, or think to ourselves, which we have convinced ourselves to be true but which are actually neither true nor false. A belief such as

"*Getting a loan from a bank is hard*" is just a belief. It is neither true nor false. It is just a belief.

Most of our beliefs are subconscious, meaning that we are not conscious of even having that belief. For example, I could venture a guess that you are probably not aware of the fact that you have a subconscious belief that tells you that if an elephant stepped on your foot it would hurt, right?

I mean, except for a small number of people in the world, chances are that you have probably never consciously thought about whether or not it would hurt if an elephant stepped on your foot, yet that belief does exist in your subconscious mind.

Much the same way, you may have a subconscious belief that the ocean water on a beach in Africa is warmer than the ocean water on a beach in Alaska. You probably never thought about these things, until I mentioned them but the crazy thing is that whether or not you're aware of it, you already have pre-programmed subconscious beliefs relating to millions of different things and you're not even aware of them.

In the example I covered before with the bank loan, the belief "XYZ *Bank is very strict about lending out money*" could be a subconscious belief that you picked up from your parents several decades ago when you were just a child and you overhead your father saying that statement to someone else. You may not even be aware of believing such a belief, but nevertheless that belief is there in your subconscious mind, affecting your thoughts and actions and affecting The Universe's ability to help you achieve your desired result.

Limiting beliefs can act like speed bumps, slowing down The Universe's ability to help you manifest what you want, and in some cases they can also act like brick walls where they completely stall your efforts and keep you trapped within the limits of your beliefs.

Within the pages of hundreds of personal development books I have read, the central message in all of them points to the fact that if we could just somehow grow aware of our own limiting beliefs and then have some way to be able to change those limiting beliefs to empowering beliefs instead, we would be able to completely change our lives.

Book after book I have read, point to limiting beliefs as the central cause of all failure in life, yet until very recently I have never seen an effective system to overcome limiting beliefs.

Up until about six months ago, the closest thing I have seen to overcoming limiting beliefs has been the power of affirmations. The use of affirmations has been written about in personal development books for decades and I've been using them for the last fifteen years to help me re-program some of the limiting beliefs that I picked up in my life growing up.

Books such as "Think and Grow Rich" state that using affirmations is one of the only ways to overcome limiting beliefs. Personally I've had some great success with affirmations, but what I have found is that while affirmations have worked wonders for me in certain areas of my life, they were largely ineffective in other areas. All in all I would say that affirmations have worked for me about 30-40% of the time. Meaning, when they do work they are 100% effective in reprogramming a limiting belief, but when they don't work they are 0% effective.

For over a decade now I've been looking for a better, more effective way to overcoming limiting beliefs and to be honest I thought that there really was no better solution than affirmations because I figured if there was something more effective then I would have heard about it by now.

Well, it turns out that I have found something that is much more effective than using affirmations. It is a method which not only allows you to identify limiting beliefs, but to also help you balance them out. The first part of identifying your limiting beliefs is actually just as important, if not more important than the second part of balancing them out.

The reason for this is because often times the limiting beliefs that are preventing us from manifesting what we want, seemingly have nothing to do with the thing we are trying to manifest. For example, you may be trying to manifest a raise at your job and the limiting belief that is slowing your progress has nothing to do with work at all. The limiting belief could simply be something like "*I do not take care of my body*" or "*I am not an honest person*".

At first it may seem very strange that a belief like "*I do not take care of my body*" should have anything to do with your ability to manifest a raise at your job, but then when we really think about it we may realize that we did promise to start exercising on a regular basis as soon as we could afford to buy a gym for our home.

In an example like this we create friction because we have a desire to get a raise at a job, but at the same time we made a promise to start exercising as soon as we could afford to do so, while also hanging onto the subconscious belief that we are the type of person who doesn't take care of their body.

If The Universe were to help us manifest a raise, we would no longer have an excuse not to exercise and then we would be going against our belief that we don't take care of our body. We don't realize this, but we do this to ourselves all the time. We choose to believe beliefs that are at odds with each other and then we wonder why we are stuck.

What I am saying is that, for example, just because we're having problems manifesting something like weight loss, doesn't mean that the limiting beliefs that are screwing us up have anything to do with weight loss. They could be related to self worth, feeling loved, be financially related or any number of other things we may not even be aware of.

I believe this is one of the reasons why affirmations don't always work. It is not that repeating a series of statements over and over again doesn't affect our subconscious mind, but rather that we may be choosing the wrong statements to repeat. Your affirmation may need to be "*I am worthy of all the love I receive in life*" and not "*I now make $10,000/month.*"

So, the issue of solving limiting beliefs requires a solution to two problems:

1. The ability to identify the limiting belief(s) creating the speed bump or brick wall that's slowing down or stalling our efforts in achieving the very specific result we desire, and;
2. The ability to "balance out" or "re-program" those limiting beliefs.

As I mentioned before, up until about six months ago I have been using affirmations to overcome limiting beliefs and affirmations can be very powerful. I've been able to manifest everything from a six-figure salary to buying the property of my dreams using nothing more than affirmations to overcome any limiting beliefs I had which were holding me back, so I don't want to take anything away from the power of using affirmations.

If you don't have access to the second method I'm going to mention in a second here, just use affirmations and you will be fine. Without any doubt you should be able to at least use the power of affirmations to be able to manifest enough money to easily afford utilizing the second method.

I mention the second method because I have found it to be very effective, but unlike affirmations it isn't free and it isn't something that I can teach you in this book. You either have to see a practitioner who is trained in this method, who can help to balance your limiting beliefs, or you can choose to become a practitioner yourself in which case you'll be able to balance out your own limiting beliefs.

This second method I'm referring to is something called PSYCH-K®. PSYCH-K® is a process by which you can identify and balance out limiting beliefs for yourself or with someone else. One of the best ways to manifest a goal in your life that has been stubbornly stuck due to some kind of limiting belief that you're not aware of is to have a session with a PSYCH-K® practitioner who will be able to help you to identify the exact limiting belief or beliefs that are slowing you down and help you to balance them out.

The beauty of the system is that it is your own subconscious mind that tells the practitioner exactly which limiting belief or beliefs that are slowing you down as well as the preferred method to use in order to balance out those limiting beliefs. In this way, PSYCH-K® is not something that is done **to you**, but rather it is something you do **with** a practitioner. In is a healing / balancing method where the practitioner is simply there to help facilitate the healing / balancing within yourself, not to offer healing from them to you.

A full understanding of PSYCH-K® and the processes involved in utilizing it to overcome limiting beliefs is beyond the scope of this book. As of the time of the writing of this book I have completed the basic PSYCH-K® practitioner training myself, mostly for the purpose of being able to do PSYCH-K® balances with myself but I don't currently offer PSYCH-K® as a service I do with others.

If in the future I may decide to offer PSYCH-K® as one of the services I offer on my site, but for now I can point you to a page on my site where you can learn more about PSYCH-K® and connect with practitioners in your area who will be able to help you with any limiting beliefs you may have.

Here is the link: http://www.paulymath.com/psych-k

Either way, regardless whether you use PSYCH-K®, affirmations or some other method to help you overcome limiting beliefs, by eliminating the limiting beliefs that are slowing you down, you are helping The Universe to use the Law of Attraction to help you manifest what you want in life in the easiest, simplest and most efficient way possible with as few speed bumps and brick walls in the way.

CHAPTER 4 - DESTINY AND FREE WILL

When we begin to consciously use the Law of Attraction to manifest our desires, we often start to see a pattern of successful manifestations in some areas of our lives while in other areas we don't. Because of this, it is sometimes easy to jump to a conclusion that The Universe is willing to help us manifest certain things but unwilling to manifest others.

I have often wondered about this myself. Is there some kind of path that we're "supposed" to be on, and if we are on this path will The Universe reward us with a life of ease and abundant manifesting abilities, while at the same time punishing us when we stray off this path by withholding the very things we desire the most?

Although it would be easy to hand over our personal power to The Universe by proclaiming that it is the ultimate power that tells us what we should and shouldn't do, I don't believe this to be true.

Even though it may seem at times that The Universe seems to favor some of our desires and makes it easier for us to manifest them, compared to others, I believe the reason for this goes back to our beliefs. When we have a desire to manifest something which also doesn't have a lot of limiting beliefs attached to it, we find it easy to engage the Law of Attraction to help us manifest what we desire.

However, when we try to manifest something that requires going outside of our limiting beliefs, it seems as if something "out there" is preventing us from achieving success. In reality, this something that is seemingly "out there" and that we sometimes personify and call The Universe, is not really "out there" at all but actually "in here". It is our own limiting beliefs that are slowing us down, not some kind of all-powerful Universe that has an agenda for our lives.

Before jumping to the conclusion that there is a Universe out there that is not co-operating with your plans to manifest something, you may want to consider that you are part of The Universe. The Universe is not some kind of separate entity outside of you. The Universe is within you, and you are within The Universe. Your desires are The Universe's desires and The Universe's desires are your desires.

When you have an experience in your life that creates a desire in your life, that desire is simultaneously your desire and The Universe's desire as well. You can't have a desire without that desire being simultaneously within The Universe at the same time.

Is it possible for us to have pointless desires though? Meaning, is it possible for us to create a desire for something in our lives that we don't really even want, or that we "shouldn't" want?

Well, there are a few things to consider here.

First of all, I'm sure you've experienced moments of time in your life when you had a desire for something, such as some kind of new toy or gadget or something you saw at a store and later on after manifesting this desire in your life you realized it wasn't really what you wanted. We've all manifested somewhat pointless things, and some of us have houses filled with "stuff" that we would now consider rather pointless.

More than anything, this actually proves that there is no judge out there called The Universe that judges us based on our desires and prevents us from manifesting things we don't need or shouldn't really want. If that was the case we wouldn't have all this stuff in our homes that we manifested on impulse, right?

I believe that it is entirely possible to manifest everything in our lives, regardless whether those things are meaningful to us or completely meaningless. The degree of manifesting difficulty doesn't seem to be correlated to the amount of deeper meaning something has in our lives. We've all manifested very meaningful things in our lives, and we've all also manifested some rather meaningless things as well.

I believe we have complete free will in being able to manifest anything we want in our lives. Besides the beliefs in our minds and everything else that encompasses who we are, I don't believe there is any other force out there that judges and decides which desires we can or cannot manifest in our lives.

Having said that, I do believe we live our lives in harmony with the desires of The Universe which we are a part of. Meaning, I believe that we are spiritual beings which live beyond the earthly desires of our bodies and I believe our desires come from a combination of desires from our Ego/Body self, our Higher Self and our Universal Self.

Our human bodies have desires that generally revolve around eating, resting, moving, procreating, experiencing physical pleasure and avoiding physical pain. Our mind/ego self also has desires which intertwine with the desires of our body self. Our Higher Self, the spiritual part of us that goes beyond our mortal body, also has desires which intertwine with the desires of our Body and Mind. And finally our Universal Self, which represents all of life has desires as well.

It is this concert, or dance of desires from the many layers of our True Self which make up our desires. When we live our lives imbalanced, satisfying only the needs of one of our selves - such as for example when we only live for the body, or such as when we ignore the body and only live for the mind - that is when our lives run into trouble. That is when our ability to manifest our desires seems to diminish in capacity because we are in effect fighting within ourselves.

When our mind desires something, but our body self tries to overthrow that desire with its own desires, we begin to battle within ourselves. Sometimes it is our body and our minds that pursue their own desires, attempting to ignore the calls of our higher spiritual self. As with any internal battle, there can never be a winner. We always lose. The only way to win, is not to fight with ourselves.

Go through your list of desires. What things on your list represent Body desires? What things on your list represent Mind/Ego desires? What things on your list represent your Higher Self/Spiritual desires? There is no need to try to balance out these desires in some mathematical way, as you may very well have a thousand Body desires for just one main Higher Self desire, but you can ask yourself if there is a part of your whole being that you are ignoring.

Bring your entire self into the picture - your body, your mind and your spirit and get every part of your True Self working together to achieve and manifest what you want. By aligning these parts of yourself, within the free will of everyday life you will discover a sense of destiny and purpose that aligns your desires with the desires of the entire Universe.

CHAPTER 5 - NON LINEAR THINKING

When we activate the Law of Attraction to manifest the things we want in our lives, we must realize that the thing we desire isn't going to always come to us in a perfectly logical and linear way. In fact, it almost never does.

Let's say for example that you decide to manifest a new job. Something more creative with a company that you enjoy working for instead of the dead-end job you have right now. Now, let's say that the logical first step would be to buy a newspaper and look in the classifieds section or to look online for job ads.

So you jump online to check out the classifieds and find no jobs that even remotely resemble what you're looking for. This goes on for several days and you start to lose faith in being able to find something worth pursuing.

Then the weekend comes up and you get invited to a BBQ, but you're feeling a bit depressed about being stuck at your current job so you're not sure if you even want to go and socialize.

While thinking about it, you have this intuitive urge that you should go anyway. While at the BBQ the host mentions to his other friend that you own a truck and that friend in turn asks you help them move. You agree but now you're regretting even showing up because you have now gotten sucked into helping move someone you barely know out of politeness.

Moving day shows up and you head over to help your new "friend" move. While there, you meet a friend of his you've never met before either and the two of you start chatting. You casually mention that you hate your job and the type of job you'd love to be doing instead. You finish helping with the move and head home.

When you get home you jump online to see the latest job postings and still find absolutely nothing worth pursuing. You now get even more depressed and start wondering if maybe your current job isn't that bad.

The next day on your way from a hellish day at work you're driving home when your phone rings. You don't recognize the number so you let it go to voicemail. Later when you get home you check your messages and the message is from your friend's - friend's - friend who you met while moving. He's calling because his girlfriend works at a company that is currently expanding in the area and they're looking to hire people for the exact position you are looking for. He wants to know whether or not you'd be willing to come in for an interview before they post the job online.

You go to the job interview, land the job and love it.

See how non-linear and illogical the path towards getting the job was? Instead of the linear / logical path we are pre-programmed to follow by common thinking - which is to jump online and start looking for job ads for example, your path towards attracting the perfect job was disguised in a weekend BBQ which led to you lending a favor to help your new friend move which then led to meeting your friend's friend which then led to him talking to his girlfriend about you and ultimately resulted in your finding your new job.

This is the way The Universe puts things together. Seldom do things get put together in a conventional, logical straight-line path. This is why many people start to utilize The Law of Attraction to attract things and then even though they are just a few feet away from success, they sabotage things by not participating in the process.

What if you decided to ignore your intuitive urge to go to the BBQ? What if you refused to help your friend's friend move? What if you didn't listen to your gut when you felt the urge to tell your new friend that you're looking for a job?

All these small and seemingly trivial events led you to land the perfect job you've been looking for but there was no logical way to predict that they would. Because we don't know the "master plan" The Universe is orchestrating to deliver what we desire, it is very difficult for us to measure our progress in terms of attracting something.

Here's another example. Imagine if you had the desire to find the next big client for your business. Someone really big that will bring you a lot of new business and that you'll thoroughly enjoy working with. You get really clear on what you want in a perfect client and the Law of Attraction begins to go to work for you.

The Universe begins to set things in motion to attract this perfect client to you. Through a series of several dozen incredible "co-incidences" spanning a three month period, the Universe has brought the perfect client to your doorstep. Normally this client never travels outside of his home in another country, but it just so happens to be that this one time only he will be attending a BBQ. The very same BBQ that you've been invited to.

Now, let's say you've been waiting for months to attract this new client and you're getting very frustrated and impatient with the Universe and the Law of Attraction because you haven't seen any progress at all. In the background, the Universe has parted seas and moved mountains on your behalf to put you and this perfect client of yours in the same place at the same time - at the BBQ.

However, because your patience wears thin you decide to give up on The Universe and the Law of Attraction and decide that starting Monday you're going back to more traditional marketing methods to find your client.

In spite of several phone calls from your friend trying to convince you to come out to the BBQ, you decide to stay home and work on your new marketing plan. You don't attend the BBQ, you don't meet your perfect client and he doesn't meet you. Neither of you, nor the host of the BBQ even realize that this "chance meeting" never transpired. All the work The Universe put into orchestrating this perfectly timed occurrence of you and your soon to be perfect client being at the same time at the same place goes down the drain because you didn't follow through to the very end.

It's easy to see the patterns that put us together or closer with the things we want when we are being told about it from a perspective that sees everything, but living our daily lives doesn't grant us the vision to see how all these things all fit together. How do we know if the Universe wants us to stay home and work on the marketing plan or to go to a BBQ? How do we know if a book we're thinking of buying and reading is the right book to buy? How do we know when to say something in a social setting and when to keep our mouth shut?

Every choice we make has consequences that are visible to us and also consequences that are invisible. You may see not going to this BBQ as making a choice between eating BBQ food or ordering in. But the real choice you are making is one where you will either meet or not meet the perfect client for your business.

The thing is that we don't know what we are really deciding when we make decisions. Do we stay home or get on the road? Do we go to the BBQ or stay at home. Do we send an email to someone or do we not? Sometimes doing something is the right thing to do, while other times not doing something is the right thing to do. But how do we know which is which?

Well, firstly the good news is that The Universe seems to work in a way where it creates multiple opportunities for us to seize that which we want. If we don't attend the BBQ, The Universe already has a backup plan. So it's not like there is this invisible decision we make or don't make and that's it, we've missed our shot of a lifetime.

The Universe knows that in most cases we will be impatient, we will ignore our intuition and gut feelings and we will tend to rely on our logical / linear thinking and our emotions more than anything. It knows that even the best laid plans by The Universe will in most cases be shattered by our lack of faith and follow through. Because of this The Universe always has a backup plan, and then another, and then another.

Of course it would be easier to just go along with the invisible plan unfolding in our lives so that the Universe wouldn't have to resort to backup plans. But how do we do this?

Well, the way to put yourself in alignment with the Universe is to believe in it, have faith in it and to trust your intuition and not just your reasoning center. The most logical path towards something is not always the shortest. Sometimes what seems to be the long way is really the short way.

Two examples from my own life can illustrate this point.

About 15 years ago I was driving home from work with my Mom and my younger brother in the car. We were approaching an intersection with two lanes. In the left lane there were four or five cars lined up waiting for the car at the very front to turn left. In the right lane the cars were going straight through the intersection on the green light.

Driving home this way I have passed this intersection hundreds of times and every single time I would get into the right lane to go straight through the intersection so that I wouldn't get stuck behind all the cars turning left. This one day though, I was in the right lane heading towards the intersection and I got the sudden urge to get into the left lane instead. It was a very strong gut feeling like I have never felt before and even though it made absolutely no logical sense at all for me to be in the left lane, I quickly jumped into the left lane anyway.

My Mom was puzzled and she wondered if I was going somewhere else instead of home since the fastest way to get home, logically speaking, was to be in the right lane. As she asked me why I'm getting in the right lane I just told her that there is something strange going on with a truck behind us.

I have no idea why I even said that, but I looked in my rear view mirror and I saw a pick-up truck about two blocks behind us. I don't know why but I kept staring in the rear-view mirror and watching as this pick-up truck was heading towards us. At this point I was stopped behind the car in front of us in the left lane as the light had turned red at the intersection ahead of us.

As the pick-up truck got closer, I could see he was accelerating and kind of swerving between the left and right lanes. For a few seconds he was half way in the left lane and as he approached my stopped car he swerved into the right lane, missing the back of my car by a few feet. He accelerated past us in the right lane and was gunning towards the intersection ahead.

31

In the right lane there was one car stopped at the red light. If I hadn't moved into the left lane, my car would have been stopped behind this one car. The pick-up truck kept accelerating towards the car in the right lane and barreled into it without even once hitting his brakes until after he hit the car. All the windows in the car that was hit blew out and a big cloud of shattered glass exploded several feet in the air. My Mom, my brother and I sat there in shock - all knowing that this could have been us if I had stayed in the right lane.

It turned out that the driver of the pick-up truck was intoxicated and was driving drunk. The car he hit belonged to a lady who walked away from the accident but I'm sure she had some really bad back and neck injuries. Her car was totaled. The back seat of her car was pressed up against the front seat. Luckily there was nobody else in her car, just her. If she had her kids in the back seat they probably would have been killed or severely injured. If it was my car that was hit, my brother who was sitting in the back seat would have suffered the same fate.

Luckily, I managed to avoid this accident by listening to my intuition and trusting it instead of my logical mind. Even though I have driven down that street and through that intersection hundreds of times before, when my intuition screamed at me to get into the left lane I just did it.

On another occasion about 8 years later, I was driving home with my wife heading down a hill we have driven hundreds of times before. Once again I was in the right lane because that was the lane I needed to be in, in order to get home. While driving in the right lane I once again got this urge to get into the left lane. I didn't ask why, I just did it.

As we came down the hill, coming around the corner we suddenly came across a mini-van, dead stopped just around the bend of the corner. It would have been really difficult to see this mini-van around this bend until the last minute and I probably wouldn't have been able to stop in time without hitting it, if I was in the right lane. It was dead stopped in the absolute worst spot you could possibly think of stopping on that downhill road.

As we passed the mini-van, I looked to my right to see why in the world this person would have dead stopped his car like that and apparently he had hit a dog. A dog must have jumped out in front of his mini-van and he hit it. The owner of the mini-van was standing in front of his mini-van, most likely in shock of what just happened. What he didn't realize is that if someone (like me) came around the corner and hit his mini-van, the mini-van would have hit him.

These are both rather extreme examples of how The Universe nudges us and communicates with us through our intuition, but these intuitive nudges don't just happen once every 8 years and they don't just happen to me. These nudges are happening to you all the time, you just may not be listening.

As you can see, there was no logical or rational reason why I was drawn to get into those left lanes at those times. It was just a gut feeling and I listened. I've had many other such events in my life where I listened to my intuition and avoided trouble, while others who ignored their intuition didn't.

In most cases, however, the intuitive feelings we have don't always present us with an immediate reason why. I mean how many accidents have I avoided which I didn't witness? It's easy to see yourself avoiding an accident when it happens right in front of you, but what if you get the intuitive insight to not get on the road at all one day? Maybe you avoided an accident but don't even realize it. I'm sure it happens all the time. Perhaps forgetting your keys in the house and having to run back inside to grab them wasn't such a bad thing. Maybe that's what The Universe did to prevent you from being in the wrong place at the wrong time.

These examples illustrate how listening to our intuition can prevent us from harm, but that is not the only time we can use our intuition. The best way to participate and harmonize your life and your decisions with those of The Universe to help you get what you want is to begin to trust your intuition, your gut, your instincts or whatever you call that part of yourself.

In fact if you study the most successful people in the world in every area of life, you will always find stories of people who are following their instincts. They may label it as instincts, or gut feelings or intuition but whatever label they give it, it's not just their reasoning center they are listening to.

Intuition is the way The Universe communicates with us It's the nudge it gives us to help us be in the right place at the right time instead of being at the wrong place at the wrong time. It's the way it communicates with us to help us get what we desire.

Because of this, one of the best ways to improve our success with the Law of Attraction is to work on developing and listening to our intuition.

Remember, the path that the Universe lays out in front of us to get us from where we are (point A) to where we want to be (point B) isn't always going to be a straight line. In fact it almost never will. We may need to make decisions and head in directions which may not seem like they are leading us on the right path at first. In the end though, if we trust our intuition, we will arrive at our destination, quicker, faster and safer than any logical, straight line path would have taken us.

CHAPTER 6 - INSPIRED ACTION

No other topic has attracted as much controversy in The Law of Attraction circles as the topic of taking action. Law of Attraction skeptics always claim that The Law of Attraction is bogus because in order to manifest anything in your life you need to take action. They state that success requires hard work and really all The Law of Attraction does is motivates people to take action. Their claim is that it is the action itself that produces results not any mysterious Law of Attraction.

On the other end of the spectrum, we have people who are under the impression that all The Law of Attraction requires is for us to make a shopping list of all the things we want to manifest in life, and then stay positive and wait for those things to appear in our lives out of thin air with no energy or effort expanded on our part.

From my experience, neither of these views are correct. The reason why I disagree with the first group of people, who simply advocate massive action as a way of creating success in our lives is because I've been there, I've tried it and it didn't work for me. I used to run a business, working 12-16 hour days, 6-7 days a week, and worked my butt off trying to get ahead. For almost two years I worked this insane schedule yet my personal income didn't increase any more than when I used to be a mid-level employee working 8 hour days with zero responsibilities of managing and running the company.

I did the "*you have to work hard and smart to succeed*" path for years and all it manifested for me was frustration and burnout. It surely didn't manifest the type of income I wanted to earn at the time.

Then, I discovered The Law of Attraction through Wallace Wattles' book "The Science of Getting Rich". As I read through the pages of this book I got really excited because the content seemed so familiar and made so much sense to me even though I had never read the book before. It was as if I was intimately familiar with the content at an intuitive or subconscious level and it had just been brought to the forefront of my consciousness.

After reading the principles taught in "The Science of Getting Rich", I immediately began implementing everything taught in the book and my income skyrocketed within a matter of months while at the same time the amount of work I did in a given week dropped as well. What I began doing instead of "hard work" was something called "taking inspired action".

"Inspired action" is not something that is easy to define objectively, as really only the person doing the action itself really knows whether or not the action is "inspired" or not. Learning to take inspired action is simple but it's not easy. The simplest way I can describe what inspired action is, would be to label it as action that you are intuitively drawn and inspired to take.

Sometimes inspired action is simply the very next action step that needs to be taken on a given path from point A to point B, but other times inspired action is taking action that may not really make any sense logically but that does produce results.

Probably the best way for a person to understand what inspired action is, is to offer some real life examples that shine a light on it.

The first example I can think of is the situation where you are given an enormous amount of work to do on a project, such as for example when you are working for a boss or a client who is constantly inundating you with more work than anyone could possibly finish in the given time period. You may have been asked to do twenty things in a given day by a client or a boss, and there is absolutely no way that you could finish all of them. Some of the tasks are rather easy to do, and you've done them before, but other tasks are not as easy.

Typically in a scenario like this, there are usually a few tasks - maybe two or three out of twenty - which are really the most important tasks that the client or boss really needs done. By tuning in intuitively you should be able to identify which of the tasks feel like they are more important compared to others. They may not be the most urgent ones either. By being able to tune in and see which of the tasks you are inspired to complete first, you can devote more focus and energy to getting those and only those tasks completed while most other people would have tried to get everything done in a mad rush to finish.

In this way, by knowing which tasks are the real important ones that must be done I have been able to handle much bigger projects with much more responsibility than most people, simply because I can typically tune in and intuitively know what to focus my energy on next.

This is the first aspect of taking inspired action - it is the process of taking action on things that you are inspired to take action on, by listening to your intuition and not your reasoning center. The inspired action is not always the most logical next step, and it is also not always the easiest or simplest action to take.

The next example of inspired action is that often times inspired action takes you on a different path than your original plan based on reason alone. For example, you may normally purchase your computer hardware and peripherals from a certain supplier. However, when it comes time to buy a new computer for your office you feel inspired to seek out a new supplier instead of going with your existing one. You have no logical reason to seek out a new supplier, but you just feel inspired to do so intuitively.

You later find out that the new supplier you are now buying your computers from ends up sending you dozens of new referrals for your business - something your former supplier never did. Later, you also find out that your previous supplier ended up going out of business two months after you would have purchased your hardware from them which means you would have been left with computer hardware without warranty.

Another example of inspired action is when you are faced with a business decision that has no clear indicator for the best course of action. You may be stuck trying to decide between two options which either both seem good or neither of them seems good. Inspired action could mean choosing one of the two options with no logical reason for the decision, or not choosing either of the two options and instead choosing to do nothing. Sometimes non-action is the best course of inspired action.

In fact, I would say that very often the biggest challenge people have with manifesting what they want is not the challenge of not taking enough action, but rather the habit of taking unnecessary and wasted action. A lot of people are addicted to taking action. It doesn't matter to them what kind of action they're taking or what kind of results that action is actually producing - they just want to be taking action.

Inspired action starts with a clearly defined goal or vision of what it is that you want to accomplish. Without a clearly defined goal or vision, there can be no inspired action because inspired action requires a purpose. If you don't have any idea what you're trying to accomplish, how can your intuition guide you towards taking the most efficient and effective action possible?

Once you have a clearly defined goal and vision of what you want to accomplish, inspired action requires patience and internal stillness to listen to your intuition, your gut, your instincts in any given situation. The right action to take at the right time will present itself.

Sometimes, the right action will be to sit still and take no action at all. This is where action-type personalities really get all upset because they don't like the idea of sitting still and not doing anything. They believe that by sitting still nothing is being accomplished but the exact opposite could be true. If your intuition is telling you to sit still for a while, then by all means sit still - that is your inspired action at that point in time.

Your inspired action may be to rest, sleep, meditate, sit still, or any number of other actions that don't seem like actions at all. These may be exactly the type of action steps that are required to get you closer to what you want and you simply just don't realize it yet.

Once you have identified the inspired action that you should be taking in a given moment, the most important thing to do is to remember that you must complete every action in what Wallace

Wattles called "*that certain way*". His description of "*that certain way*" is simply that the action is completed with the vision and intention of successfully completing that action for the purpose of achieving your goal or outcome.

Meaning, if you're inspired to read a book as your inspired action then read that book with the intention of achieving your goal or outcome. If your inspired action is to rest, then rest with the intention of achieving your goal. Be clear on your outcome and purpose for that outcome and stay focused on it.

CHAPTER 7 - CHARGING UP YOUR ENERGY

The next thing we need to look at in terms of manifesting the things that you desire is to look at the energy and power levels that you are attracting with.

Firstly let's define the "energy" or "power" I am referring to here. The energy/power I'm referring to is not any type of energy that we experience in the physical world. I'm not referring to electricity, sound, light or magnetism or anything like that. All of those types of energy are manifestations of the more "spiritual" energy I'm referring to which in its unmanifested form is invisible to our senses.

However, even though this energy is invisible in its unmanifested form, it is absolutely possible for us to harness it and build it up using physical world techniques. There are two main techniques that I have discovered and used for directly harnessing this power, and several supportive techniques to amplify it.

The first technique may sound simplistic, but it is very powerful. Many people dismiss it for its simplicity, but those who utilize it find that they are able to manifest what they desire much more quickly and with more accuracy. By accuracy I simply mean that they manifest exactly what they wanted, and not simply something similar - such as for example manifesting a very specific year/model/make of car with very specific features and color, and not just manifesting a car in general.

This first technique I simply call "Creating Desire".

Creating Desire can be done in many different ways, but regardless of the techniques you use to create desire, the main requirement is to develop **meaning** for the thing you desire in your life. It is through the development of **meaning** that we create desire. All the different techniques we use to develop desire are worthless if they don't develop meaning first.

Let's use an example so that it's easier to understand. Let's take the technique of visualizing what we want as a way of building up desire for it. All we need to do is close our eyes, and imagine the thing that we want to build desire for and simply by visualizing it in our minds we are automatically increasing our desire for it.

However, even though imagining something builds up desire energy to a degree, it is not as powerful as if we start to attach meaning to it. For example, imagining owning a brand new BMW® does produce some desire energy, but visualizing yourself driving to a business meeting in your BMW® and meeting a prospective customer who comments on your nice car adds meaning to the visualization. It starts to build the "why" behind why you may want the car in the first place.

Imagine for a second taking a new BMW® for a Sunday drive on a sunny day with the top down and the wind blowing through your hair. As you make your way towards the beach you can't help to notice that the sky is perfectly blue with just a few small white clouds. Your favorite song comes on the radio and you turn it up.

See how visualizing more specific details about what you want in the car begins to add meaning to it? You start to associate freedom with owning that BMW®. You start to associate sunny days with that BMW®. You start to associate taking a day off and taking a nice, relaxing drive in your favorite car with that BMW®. It is those associations that mean something to you specifically, and that meaning is what creates desire.

Visualizing what you desire in a sort of 3D virtual model in your mind, disconnected from you and your life doesn't produce a lot of desire energy because you haven't associated any meaning to it yet. You need to associate meaning to it.

A while back I participated in a contest which would allow me to win a brand new MacBook® Pro laptop if I won first place in the contest. The contest was about half over before I started participating, but immediately after entering the contest I began using this exact visualization tool to develop meaning and desire for the laptop.

I didn't just visualize a MacBook® Pro. I visualized myself using a MacBook® Pro to do video editing and to start posting videos on my Blog. I visualized myself using the laptop in my living room while watching TV with my wife, and also taking it outside to be able to Blog outside in the sunshine. I visualized all sorts of situations where I would be able to use this laptop to do my Blogging work without being tied down to my desktop computer.

By the time the contest was in the last few days of competition I had built up such a desire for that laptop that I probably would have gone out and bought one if I didn't win the contest. In the end I placed first in the contest and ended up winning the laptop. There is a video I created and uploaded on my Blog which talks about how I used visualization as one of the tools I used to win this competition. This concept of visualizing and associating meaning to our desires is very powerful, but many people dismiss it because it is so simplistic.

There are many other ways of building desire. Some people prefer to create vision boards where they print out or cut out pictures from magazines and post them on a cork board representing the things they want to manifest in their lives. Other people prefer to write things out on a list or by writing out a perfect day in a journal. It doesn't really matter which tool you use, as they can all be equally effective as long as you use them to associate meaning to the thing that you are attempting to manifest.

If you want to manifest a new job, don't just write down "New Job" on a TODO list and leave it at that. This is a very weak way to manifest a desire. Put some energy behind it by associating meaning behind your desire. Why do you want a new job? What will it mean to you? What will it mean to your family? What will it mean to your future? What will it mean to your new co-workers? Who's lives will you change? etc. Start asking yourself these types of questions and visualize all the benefits and all the meaning associated with your desires.

Remember it is the **meaning** behind the thing you are trying to manifest which creates the desire, not the thing itself. A BMW® or a new job or any other thing or event, in and of itself has no meaning. It is you who associates meaning to it. Of course it may seem like a brand new BMW® would automatically mean more you to you than a less expensive car, for example, but that is only because you associate more meaning to it - consciously or unconsciously. To some people in the world, a BMW® has no meaning while for others it has all the meaning in the world.

That is what makes this reality we live in so wonderful. We are free to choose what holds meaning for us. The mistake some people make is that they think that objects and events out there already have meaning, and all we have to do is discover the ones that mean the most and try to attain them. This is a mistake. Nothing has any meaning except that which we give it.

You may have been raised to associate more meaning to certain things, but you are always free to "re-wire" your mind to associate meaning towards anything you want. Often times when we meet new people or get around new social circles we tend to absorb their energy as ours and we take on the meaning they have associated to things as our own.

For example when couples start dating, the meaning one person associates to something that is very important to them will often rub off on the other person. I'm sure you know couples who are examples of this, if not yourself. As soon as the couple starts dating all of a sudden they both start caring about things that the other person cares about even if it didn't mean anything to them before they met.

This happens because we tend to absorb the meaning others around us associate with things, but it is also possible - and probably preferable - to create and associate your own meaning towards things you desire.

For example, if nobody around you values or associates a lot of meaning towards being an entrepreneur, but that is something you desire to be, then by all means use visualization and any other similar tools to develop meaning and desire behind being an entrepreneur. Don't wait for someone else to infect you with their contagious entrepreneur energy - create your own!

The second technique for creating desire builds on top of the work you've done with meaning. What it entails is creating energy more directly around the thing you desire. This technique is a bit harder to explain as it will be different for everyone involved, but essentially what you want to do is to put yourself in a peak state energy wise and then while you are in that peak state - visualize the thing you desire so that you link the thing you desire with that peak state.

For example, one way I have done this before is by using my jogging time on a treadmill. During my run on a treadmill, I will reach a point in my run where I will turn on one of my favorite songs and I'll turn up the speed on the treadmill. As I reach a running pace, with my favorite song playing I can feel all this energy coursing through my body. It is at that peak state where I feel awesome and invincible that I will visualize the thing that I desire to manifest and I'll imagine already having or owning it and how awesome it will feel.

There are many different ways to get yourself in this peak state. It can be done through exercise, dancing, by watching an inspiring movie or watching your favorite sports team win. Or perhaps you feel this feeling the most by simply going for a walk or by feeding pigeons at the park. It really doesn't matter what you do, but essentially the idea is to take something that you already "own" in your life that makes you feel awesome and use it to get yourself in that high peak state and then visualize what you desire while in that state.

Going back to my running example, if I wanted to manifest an extra $10,000 in my life, I might use the word "10K" as a mental chant I do while running. I'll get into a comfortable running state, turn on my favorite song, crank up the treadmill, and while I do my short sprint I'll mentally chant the words "10k, 10k, 10k, 10k..." in my mind over and over again and visualize how awesome it would be to have an extra $10,000 in my life. Of course I'm using a monetary value just as an example, you can use this for anything you wish to manifest such as better health, a new relationship, some kind of object or event, or whatever else you want.

So essentially, these two main techniques work together. The first one associates meaning to what you want to manifest and thus increases your desire energy towards it. The second technique takes something you already do or have in your life that puts you in an amazing state and uses the energy of that state to add more desire towards the thing you want to manifest. These are both very simple, yet very powerful techniques I have used personally to manifest a lot things in my life.

There are also a number of smaller, supporting techniques that are associated with these. Essentially they involve doing things which either help you gain clarity as to the meaning behind your life, or they increase your physical energy in life.

For example, taking a course, going to a seminar, watching a movie or simply reading a book which inspires you and brings more meaning to your life in general, will help you with your ability to associate more meaning to more specific things. What I mean by this is that someone who associates a lot of meaning to their life in general, has a greater ability to create meaning around the things they want to manifest.

On the other hand, someone who doesn't really see a lot of meaning to their life as a whole will often find it harder to create as much meaning towards something else. Because of this, it is always beneficial to be constantly working on finding meaning in your life in general and developing your desire and will to live.

Also, as far as the second technique of visualizing that which you desire during peak state events in your life is concerned, the magnitude with which you are capable of creating peak states affects your ability to use this technique.

If for example you have not yet learned how to get into a peak excited state through some means, such as cheering for your favorite sports team, exercising, dancing, taking a walk, listening to music, reading a book, watching a movie, playing a game, playing an instrument, playing with your pets or your children, or something that brings you joy in your life, then it will be harder for you to apply this second technique with any effectiveness.

In such a case it may be beneficial to first find something that gets you excited and makes you feel good, even if it's just for a few minutes or even for a few seconds. Maybe it's a song you really enjoy listening to. Whatever it may be, find something that puts you in a peak state and use that state to visualize what you wish to manifest.

Then, also seek out other opportunities to get yourself into this state on more occasions. If this is something that is difficult for you to reach, you can try using crowd dynamics as a way of accomplishing this.

For example, I once attended a professional hockey game where the crowd was absolutely electrified when our home town hockey team skated onto the ice. The cheering, the laser light show, and the music created an amazing energy atmosphere that everyone in the building could feel. In moments like that, when you are in a peak state because the whole entire building is in a peak state, use that moment to visualize what you want.

Of course you don't have to go to a hockey game to experience this. Just go to any gathering of people where everyone is happy and excited and celebrating, such as a movie, a parade or anything else your imagination can think of. This way, you can essentially feed off the energy of the crowd to bring your energy levels up and then while you are in a peak state - visualize your object of desire.

One final thing that I would like to mention. Our physical bodies are very much linked to this last technique. Meaning, by taking better care of your body you will improve its capacity to feel good and to raise the level of peak state you can attain. When our bodies are hurting, or sick, it can be more difficult - although not impossible - to create peak states, which is why any kind of activity you do which helps to maintain and improve the health of your body ultimately also supports your ability to manifest other things in your life as well.

CHAPTER 8 - SELFISH SELFLESSNESS

If we all become rich, who's going to clean the toilets?

It is statements like this that point to a deep human belief that we can't all experience the abundance that The Universe provides for us because if we did, it would ruin the world. In reality, it is actually the exact opposite that is true.

Our upbringing teaches us that it is better to be selfless than it is to be selfish, or that it is better to give than it is to receive. The challenge with statements like this is that they are half-truths. It is not better to give or receive - they are equal parts of the same thing.

One of the challenges you may run into as you experience success with manifesting your desires is this issue of feeling guilty about possibly being what we in our society call "selfish". The premise of "selfishness" is flawed because it assumes The Universe is a zero-sum game, where you having more abundance means someone else having less. In reality, the opposite is true. You having more abundance in your life actually means more abundance for everyone.

As you begin to listen to your intuition and your inspired desires, you will need to develop the trust that your seemingly "selfish" desires are actually exactly what the world needs. Anytime you come from a place of abundance, from a place of love and the desire to have more of both of those in your life, you are creating more for everyone else in the world at the same time.

For example, by manifesting the perfect relationship in your life, you automatically create more joy for everyone around you. By manifesting wealth and financial abundance in your life, you automatically create more abundance in the world.

Conversely, trying to block the desire for more abundance and more love in your life creates more lack in the world for everyone. The natural tendency for the universe is to grow and expand, and it is natural for us to want the same in our lives. By coming into alignment with who we really are, we tune into the desires of the whole Universe and no desire is trivial and unimportant.

For example, let's say that you have a deep desire to start comic book collecting. To some, the act of spending money on something like a comic book would be labeled as "wasting" money on unimportant things - as compared to, for example, something like donating money towards ending gang violence in underprivileged neighborhoods.

Most people would logically argue that donating to a cause such as ending violence is more "important" than spending money on a comic book? Someone in our society who says "*I can't donate $200 towards your cause, because I'm on my way to the comic book store where I have picked out $200 worth of comic books I'll be buying,*" would most likely be labeled as "selfish".

However, what if there are thousands of young kids in neighborhoods dominated by gang violence who express themselves through comic book art, and by buying those comic books we are actually supporting their artistic expression which will help them to help themselves to not only leave such a neighborhood, but also to inspire others to express themselves artistically and create lives of abundance?

What I have realized in my life is that by listening to my intuition and pursuing the desires which I feel come from my Higher Self, I help the world in a selfless way, even though I pursue those desires with complete selfishness.

It's kind of a backwards concept to consider at first, but what I'm saying is that the most selfless thing we can do for the world is to become crystal clear as to what are our most selfish desires - meaning those that come from our Higher Self - and then pursue them. By doing that we will create more love and more abundance in our own lives and in the lives of everyone else.

It may sound contrary to what is normally taught by our society, but we are all much better off focusing on "fixing" ourselves, than trying to "fix" everyone else out there.

There is no better way to increase the overall level of abundance in the world, than by creating more abundance in your own life.

There is no better way to improve the overall health of the world, than by improving your own health.

There is no better way to spread and teach the concepts of The Law of Attraction, than by learning and applying them yourself.

This is the paradox that limits a lot of people when trying to manifest the life they desire. There is this misconception that somehow by being miserable, you leave more "happiness" on the table for others to enjoy - or that by living a life of poverty, you are creating more "wealth" for others. It is actually the opposite of that. Every person that elevates their level of wealth in the world, automatically creates even more wealth for others.

The thing to understand here is that somehow we are all wired to be inspired to pursue different things. It may seem like if everyone had total financial abundance, we would all overcrowd the same resort and there would be nobody left in the resort to work there because we would all be rich. In reality, not everyone is inspired to be rich. For some people, their inspiration is not to build financial wealth but to be a professor, building wealth in the form of wisdom. For others it is to be an athlete. For others it is to sing or to act or to dance.

The Universe somehow organizes itself in a way where if we all just pursued our truest, deepest desires, there would be perfect harmony.

It may seem like if everyone had abundance, nobody would be left to clean the toilets but that is not true. Somehow The Universe would arrange things in such a way as to create people with the desire for janitorial work, or someone would invent a self-cleaning toilet, or some other thing would be created which would take care of the "who will clean the toilets" problem.

Don't concern yourself with such issues. It's not your "job" to try to anticipate whether or not what your heart desires is going to lead towards the eradication of some kind of job position out there.

It's kind of like how decades ago people were scared that robots are going to come in and replace their jobs in the car factory and everyone will be unemployed. Did that happen? Did robots come in and replace factory workers? Yes, some jobs have been replaced by robots but many more created. Now we have other jobs such as those for the people who engineer the robots and who fix the robots and yet other jobs have been created in other sectors where people have moved out of the factory setting and into a more service-oriented industry.

The same thing will happen with everything else in our lives. As we create more abundance, we will create more desires for other more intricate forms of abundance.

CHAPTER 9 - THE INTENTION BRIDGE

As human beings we are equipped by a number of different senses. The five senses which we are all familiar with are the senses of sight, hearing, touch, smell and taste. For each one of the senses, we also understand what we must do in the physical world in order to communicate with those senses.

For example, if we want to communicate the energy of "Congratulations" when a friend of ours has achieved something meaningful to them, we can say "Congratulations" to them communicating this energy through the sense of hearing. We could send them a card which says "Congratulations" on it and with their sense of sight they will read the card and understand what we are communicating.

We can give them a hug, or a high-five or shake their hand and communicate "Congratulations" through the sense of touch. We could even engage the senses of taste and smell by taking them out for a celebratory meal to "Congratulate" them that way.

As humans, we are very aware of our five senses because we experience and interpret our lives through them. Most of us favor one or two of these senses and experience and interpret our lives mostly through those senses.

For example, some people are more visual than others. They are more affected by seeing something than by hearing about it, while others are more partial to the sense of hearing. They are much more affected by hearing something than by seeing it. Others yet are more affected by the sense of touch than others, and they prefer to be able to touch things and hold them in their hands in order to fully experience them.

What's interesting about the five senses is that the sense which we typically favor is also usually the same sense that we expect those around us to favor as well. For example, as a visual person we unconsciously expect others to interpret life and be affected by visual information as well. We try to "illustrate" our ideas to others and "show" them what we want to communicate so that they can "see" what we are trying to communicate.

Unfortunately, not everyone in our lives will favor the same senses. A visually oriented husband may attempt to "show" his wife that he loves her through many visually stimulating means, but if his wife favors the sense of touch, the only communications she will ultimately respond to is that which involves touch. Instead of painting her a picture, or giving her a card she can see, the husband is going to have much better luck giving his wife a hug.

The same thing happens when you have a person who favors the sense of touch and they always want to hug everyone or shake their hand to show affection or communicate something as simple as "Congratulations" or "Good Job", but what they don't realize is that some people don't need a hug or a hand-shake - they need to hear the words "Congratulations" or "Good Job" spoken to them, or a visual display of those energies for those who are visual.

Our natural tendency is to interpret life through our first five senses and to also favor one or perhaps two of these five senses. Our tendency also is to ignore or at least de-value any form of communication or interaction with the world which doesn't involve the senses which we favor.

To improve your ability to manifest the life you desire, you must realize that there are many forms of energy out there. Energy does not only exist in the forms which our senses are attuned to. For example, radio waves travel in a form of energy which is unperceivable to our senses. We can't see radio waves, we can't hear them, we can't touch or smell or taste them.

However, radio waves do exist. They are just one of many types of invisible energy which we have only just mastered in the last hundred years. Our technology has allowed us to create devices which can take sound (a form of energy we can perceive), transform it into radio waves (a form of energy that is invisible to our five senses), send that energy across great distances, and then to transform that radio wave energy back into a form of energy we can perceive again - sound.

When we turn on the radio, we can hear the spoken words or the sound of music, but that voice and music doesn't originate from the radio. It originates somewhere else on the planet which transmits this energy using the invisible energy of radio waves.

The spectrum of energy which is invisible to us is great. In fact, our human senses only encapsulate a very tiny fraction of the energy spectrum and a very large portion of energy is completely invisible to us.

As I mentioned before, for the most part, people ignore and dismiss anything that they cannot perceive using the five senses. What's even worse is that even with the five senses we have, most of us largely favor just one or possibly two of those senses. Any other types of energy we are exposed to in the world, we mostly ignore.

To improve your ability of being able to manifest the life of your dreams, you must firstly accept the fact that there are forms of energy out there which are real and which do exist, but which you cannot perceive with your five senses. Intention is such a form of energy. It does exist, it is very real, but we can't perceive it with the first five human senses, and so most of us simply ignore it.

For example, if a situation arises in which we become angry and we really intend to hurt someone, and we walk up to them with the intention of hitting them but just before we are able to do it, someone else walks into the room and we stop ourselves short of taking physical action - it is easy to believe that "nothing happened". Meaning, we dismiss our intention to hurt someone as "nothing".

In the same way we can intend to quit a job which we hate, but we don't do anything about it except maintain this intention of quitting while we wait to see what happens in the workplace before we decide to take action. Then, a few weeks later we get passed over for a promotion, which goes to a less skilled candidate (in our opinion) and we get angry because that should have been our promotion. This finally drives us to take action and we quit.

What we don't realize in such a situation is that our intention of wanting to quit is a form of energy that may be invisible but that doesn't mean that it doesn't exist. The very reason we may have been passed over for the promotion could have been because of that intention energy of wanting to quit. We may wonder, how that could be since maybe we didn't do anything differently, and haven't spoken to anyone about wanting to quit - but I assure you that the energy of intending to quit is very real and it very much affects what happens in the "real" world even if we don't express it through action.

To really become a person who manifests the life of their dreams, we must acknowledge the existence and the amazing power which intention plays in our universe. It is an invisible form of energy, but it is very powerful. Dismissing it as "nothing" can be disastrous in your life.

Make a study of the energy of intention. By studying what others have discovered, theorized and proven about the energy of intention, we can begin to really utilize it in our lives for good. There are many books, studies, videos and other forms of study material which we can learn about, which refer to the energy of intention. By default, if we don't study this energy we will ignore it because we always ignore that which we don't believe to exist.

I will cover a few examples of the studies into the energy of intention here to get you started, but I strongly advise you not to rely on this information alone as your lone source of information on the energy of intention. There is a vast amount of information on this topic with new experiments and new information being done every day. Stay on top of this information and it will help to improve your manifesting skills because your belief in the energy of "intention" will help you to harness it.

The Double Slit Experiment

Perhaps one of the more famous experiments in modern science which you may want to look into is the Double Slit Experiment. The Double Slit Experiment is a very simple and easy to reproduce experiment with implications which are not so easy to explain.

Essentially, the experiment shows that small particles, such as a single electron, seem to act as both a wave (a quality of energy) and as a particle (matter). It is as if the electron - a building block of matter - is both energy and matter at the same time. What's even more interesting is that the introduction of an observer seems to be the cause of the electron "collapsing" from a wave (energy) into a particle (matter).

Of course there are many different interpretations of this experiment and there are physicists much brighter than I out there trying to explain what is happening, but my understanding and belief in regards to this experiment is that it is our energy of intention which causes the electron to "collapse" from a form of energy into a particle of matter.

If this is so, it points to the realization that our intentions essentially "cause" or "create" the very reality which we see around us. Without consciousness being there to observe, the physical reality we experience around us would simply cease to exist in the form of matter. It would revert back to a state of energy.

A few simple searches on the Internet related to this experiment will connect you with written texts, reports, videos and discussions about this experiment and what it means to the very nature of the reality we live in.

One thing I will note here though, is that many people interpret this experiment according to their personal beliefs. So, if you come across an article written by someone who does not personally believe or want to believe in the possibility of an energy like "intention" existing, and being a "cause" or having influence on the very fabric of our reality, they will interpret the experiment in a way which dismisses this possibility. Study at least a few different perspectives on this experiment and then decide on your own.

Visualization and Athletic Performance

Another example where intention energy plays a role in affecting the outcome of physical reality is in the field of professional sports and athletics. In today's world of professional sports and athletics, visualization is a key component of training.

Visualization is not something that one or two athletes use out there from time to time when they feel like it in their spare time. Visualization is a tool that almost all athletic coaches are using with their athletes which is taken as seriously as physical training and diet.

Many experiments involving athletes and athletic performance have been done over the years and what these experiments clearly demonstrate is that visualization affects athletic performance. In the book "The Intention Experiment", the author refers to experiments which show increases in muscle strength of 16.5% simply due to the process of visualizing a strength training regiment, as compared to increases of 30% in those who actually did strength training and 0% for those who did neither. Other experiments mentioned in this book point to athletes who significantly improve their performance in activities like sprinting, cycling, swimming and virtually any other form of physical activity by utilizing visualization as part of their training program.

Skeptics dismiss these findings stating that visualization is just something athletes do to make themselves feel better, and argue that it doesn't actually "do" anything to improve performance.

What they don't realize is that athletes who compete at the professional level in professional sports or who compete in the Olympics are trained by their coaches with a strict training regiment on a very focused and controlled schedule with only so much time available for training.

If visualization did not work, athletic coaches wouldn't waste their precious training time with it. Athletes wouldn't waste their time with it either. It is not like they have all this free time to waste on ineffective training methods. Athletes and athletic coaches utilize visualization - a form of intention energy - because they know it works.

There are volumes of information available on this topic. Look into it, study it and see for yourself how intention energy has been and continues to be a huge factor in improving athletic performance. Understanding the implications that this has on our reality can make a huge shift in helping you become more skilled at manifesting your intentions.

If athletes can improve their performance, and even affect their strength simply by intending and visualizing it to be so, and without actually "doing" anything in this physical reality - is it so farfetched to believe that there is this energy out there called "intention energy" which has the ability to affect our physical universe?

Medical Miracles

Another area of study which has experimented with the energy of intention is the field of medicine and health. Perhaps no other area of life becomes as important to us as health when we become ill or are facing the potential of death. At first, during such circumstances we mostly turn to modern medicine for help, but when modern medicine falls short of helping us, many people turn to something else.

In such circumstances, many people turn to prayer - another form of intention energy - to ask for help in the healthy recovery of a loved one who is sick. In fact, many doctors who are typically the most skeptical of something as invisible as the energy of intention will often tell the family members to pray for their loved ones in very difficult circumstances.

There have been many miracle stories of individuals who have recovered from serious medical conditions which the doctors told them they would never recover from, and who attribute this recovery to the power of intention. There have been countless experiments and studies done which show that the power of prayer has had a significant effect on the recovery of sick individuals.

If you look into this area of study and see some of the many examples of people who have turned to the energy of intention as a source of healing, you may be very surprised as to how common this is.

Wealth Building

Another area of study which shows countless examples of intention energy being used, is the area of wealth building. Study wealthy individuals, read their biographies and books written by them, and you will find a common thread. You will find that a large percentage of them utilize intention energy to build their wealth, even if they don't necessarily label it using those words.

For example, one night in 1987, Canadian comedian Jim Carrey drove up to Mulholland Drive up in the Hollywood hills in his old Toyota. At the time he was a struggling comic. While there, he dreamed and visualized a successful future for himself and wrote himself a check for $10 million, dating it for Thanksgiving Day 1995 and added a note at the bottom saying "for acting services rendered."

By the time Thanksgiving Day 1995 arrived, Jim Carrey's success in films such as "Ace Ventura: Pet Detective", "The Mask", and "Dumb & Dumber" had made him one of the most successful stars in Hollywood with an asking price of $10-$20 million per picture.

Bruce Lee is another famous movie star who understood the power of intention, not just with his martial arts but also when it came to business and success. As a struggling actor Bruce Lee wrote himself a letter in 1969 which said:

"__My Definite Chief Aim__, I, Bruce Lee, will be the first highest paid Oriental super star in the United States. In return I will give the most exciting performances and render the best quality in the capacity of an actor. Starting in 1970 I will achieve world fame and from then onward till the end of 1980 I will have in my possession $10,000,000. I will live the way I please and achieve inner harmony and happiness."

~ Bruce Lee

Bruce Lee's untimely death in 1973 cut his life short, but just months after his death the blockbuster movie "Enter the Dragon" elevated Bruce Lee to the level of an international superstar as an actor.

Bruce Lee's letter, stating his "Definite Chief Aim" demonstrates his belief in setting an intention and is written in a form taught in the book "Think and Grow Rich", which is one of the most popular and successful books on the topic of becoming rich and wealth building.

It doesn't take a lot of effort to dig into the biographies of wealthy and successful individuals to find this common thread of utilizing intention to manifest riches and wealth in life. From my own personal studies on the subject I have found that a large percentage of successful individuals utilize a process of engaging the energy of intention to build their massive wealth, and openly attribute their success to it. Many others utilize the energy of intention without necessarily labeling it as such, or realizing they are doing it.

Some wealthy individuals automatically visualize that which they desire to manifest, yet if you were to ask them if they've ever heard of or utilized visualization, they wouldn't know what you're talking about. See, a lot of times successful individuals do things automatically and so they don't realize they are even doing such things and they also assume everyone else does the same thing.

For example, you may ask a multi-millionaire *"Have you ever used visualization as a tool to building your wealth?"* and they may answer *"No, I don't do visualization."* However, if you inquire further and ask, *"Did you know you were going to be a millionaire when you were younger?"*, you may be surprised to hear them say *"Oh yeah, I saw myself as a millionaire living in a beautiful house, driving an exotic car every since I was a kid."*

As you can see, sometimes in order to really study successful people we need to learn what they actually do, not just what they say they do. For example, Bruce Lee may have never written a book on the subject of utilizing intention manifestation as an energy to manifest becoming a successful international superstar, but by reading his letter we can clearly see that he must have believed in this energy in order to write such a letter.

Make a study of successful people and if you look closely, you will see countless examples of people using tools such as visualization, prayer, meditation and many others as a way to harness the energy of intention to manifest success in their lives.

In fact, if you look closely enough you will realize that without the power of intention, there can be no success. Whether we are consciously aware of it or not, we all use the power of Intention in our lives every waking moment.

Study Intention and Use Intention Consciously

The more you study these examples and many other examples where Intention energy affects the very fabric of our reality, the more powerful you will become in your abilities to harness the power of intention to manifest the life you want.

Studying this energy of intention makes it real in your life, as by default it is an invisible energy no different from radio waves. Radio waves cannot be seen or heard by our regular senses, but we can see the effect of these "invisible" waves once they are manifested into a form of energy (sound) which we can sense with our sense of hearing. Once we "hear" the radio, it becomes very real and it's easy to accept radio waves as "real". What if you had to try to explain radio waves to a group of people who have never heard of such things and you didn't have a radio to "prove" to them their existence?

Intention energy works the same way. Except that instead of a radio which transforms radio waves into sound waves which we can hear, intention energy transforms into the very reality we experience with all of our senses without the need of a radio receiver. It just happens automatically and that is why we don't realize it is actually happening.

Your heart is beating right now, but you are not consciously intending to make your heart beat in this very moment - are you? Your heart beats, because of your unconscious intention for it to keep beating because you have the intention of staying alive. You are not aware of it, but something is the root cause of your heart still beating and that causes is intention energy.

Once you really understand the incredible power of intention, you will have a new appreciation for it and you will understand that it isn't just the things that we "do" in the world that affect the world, but also the things which we "intend" as well.

CHAPTER 10 - THE LAST STAND

When we first start to become consciously aware of the Law of Attraction, we begin to create events in our lives that act as personal "proof" that the Law of Attraction works. We set a goal to find a new job, and the very next day someone calls us with a job offer. We create a desire to come up with $300 to pay for some bill that needs paying and a friend comes out of nowhere and returns $300 he's owed us for years without us even having to ask. Anyone who's been using the Law of Attraction in their lives will surely know what I mean by these events.

These events feel like "winks" from The Universe and they're very inspiring and exciting to experience in our lives. However, what happens when we see the exact opposite happening in our lives? What about when we set an intention to manifest something in our lives and we get all excited about it, and perhaps even manifest a few supportive "winks" from The Universe, but then we hit a brick wall of challenges?

Often times we find ourselves in situations where it almost seems like the Universe is sending us mixed signals. We set an intention to manifest a new job and the very next day we get a phone call from a friend who works for a company that is expanding and looking for new people. We get excited and go in for an interview. The interview goes well and we are all excited and grateful for the amazing opportunity the Universe has brought to our doorstep. We wait to hear back and finally the phone rings. Except instead of hearing the good news, we find out that the position has been filled by someone else. It feels like a devastating blow.

We then start looking for another job and send out a few dozen resumes but hear nothing back. We start to wonder if the Universe is trying to tell us something. Maybe we're not supposed to get a new job right now?

The same type of thing may happen with money. We set an intention to manifest $10,000 to start off our long term savings account. At first things seem to go well. Within a few weeks we manifest an extra $500 from some extra work we pickup somewhere and we open up our new savings account. A month later we get a bonus at work and now we're up to $1,500 in our new savings account and things are looking promising. Then, yet another $250 shows up as birthday gifts. We are now up to $1,750 and we start getting excited at how quickly things are starting to add up.

Then, out of nowhere the water heater in our home breaks down and we have no choice but to get it replaced. What's worse is that the plumber also finds some other problems with our plumbing which are probably the reason the heater broke down so quickly in the first place. Sure enough, once the repairs are done we're staring at an invoice for $1,732. Now we're back to square one. How depressing!

Have you ever had these kinds of things happen to you? One minute we're thanking The Universe for supporting us and aligning the stars in our favor, and the next minute we're cursing at the heavens because all of a sudden all progress comes to a grinding halt and we take a few steps backwards.

In situations like this, I have a found myself and many of my friends and coaching clients questioning whether the path we are on is the right path. Meaning, when things in our lives don't work out the way we wanted them to, we start to interpret this as a message from The Universe that maybe we shouldn't be pursuing that path.

For example, we are inspired to find a new job but the job market "out there" beats us up and spits us out and we start to wonder if maybe we should just stay where we are and learn to be happy. Or we get inspired to start a new business, and in the beginning we start to see some support from The Universe, but then all of a sudden it seems like things aren't going so well anymore and we start wondering if running our own business is the right path for us. Thoughts like these enter our minds:

"Maybe the Universe doesn't want us to do this."

"Maybe it wasn't meant to be."

"Maybe we're not supposed to do this, or at least not yet."

"If I was meant to do this, it would be much easier."

etc.

I have often wondered the same thing in my life. In fact I have often used this "evidence" of things not working out as a sign that perhaps I should be doing something else. I mean, if it was meant to be, then it should be pretty easy right?

Wrong.

As I have similarly mentioned in a previous chapter about beliefs, making the assumption that The Universe guides us by throwing obstacles in our way, may very well be the biggest mistake we can make when learning to use the Law of Attraction in our lives.

The Universe guides us internally through an internal guidance system. We know when we are in alignment with The Universe when we feel inspired, excited and sometimes maybe a little bit scared or nervous about going after that which we are inspired to pursue.

That is how The Universe communicates with us, through internal feelings and glimpses of insight, not by manifesting problems in our lives, or by preventing us from attaining or achieving that which we are inspired to pursue.

If you are inspired to start a new business, and you encounter resistance towards achieving that goal, ask yourself *"Is the resistance coming from within me, or is it coming from 'out there'?"*

If you're still just as inspired to pursue your dream of running a business, but the world "out there" just isn't quite cooperating with you right now, then that resistance is coming from your beliefs, not from The Universe. It is your subconscious limiting beliefs manifesting these challenges, testing your courage and your perseverance to follow your inspirations.

Many of us already intuitively know this, but a tiny part of our mind wonders if perhaps The Universe is orchestrating these challenges. That little tiny part of our mind weakens our resolve and makes it much more difficult to manifest our inspirations. It's one thing to go after something we want and overcome the obstacles and challenges required to achieve or attain it, but it's quite another to try to face those obstacles and challenges with a doubtful mind which isn't even sure we should be pursuing the desire in the first place.

That little part of our mind is much more destructive and disempowering to our inspirations than any challenges or obstacles that our limiting beliefs can throw at us, and that is why this single insight and realization can have a huge impact on your Law of Attraction manifesting abilities.

Decide, right now, to never look at any obstacle or challenge that you face in the outside world as any kind of indicator from The Universe that you shouldn't be pursuing that which you are inspired to pursue. If you're inspired to find a new job, don't take a rejection letter from a company that decided against hiring you as a sign from The Universe. Consider it a test of will from your limiting beliefs. The biggest power your limiting beliefs hold over you is their ability to inject doubt into your mind.

They know that they don't stand a chance against your inspirations. They know that no matter how many obstacles they manifest and throw in your way, you will overcome them with increasing speed and ease, but if your limiting beliefs can trick you into thinking that perhaps you shouldn't be pursing your inspirations in the first place, then they have already won the battle.

This single insight is by far the biggest mistake most people make when learning to manifest their inspirations. They interpret challenges and setbacks as some kind of message from The

Universe. The Universe will speak to you internally, through your intuition, not by inspiring you to do something and then putting up road blocks against it.

The Final Act of Defiance

As a final act of desperate defiance, there is one more trick that your limiting beliefs may pull from under their sleeve and throw at you. When they see that you are no longer tricked by the illusion that the challenges your limited beliefs are throwing at you are just a test of your will to pursue your inspirations, there is one final thing your limiting beliefs may try to throw at you.

Remember that the ultimate weapon of your limiting beliefs is doubt. So the final weapon they may throw at you is to make you try to doubt this final insight itself.

Your limiting beliefs may throw some of these thoughts at you:

"What if this is wrong though. What if The Universe does communicate with us by throwing obstacles in our way?"

"What if the Universe does communicate to use by creating challenges in our lives?"

I hope by now just by reading these words your intuition feels the falsehood of these statements, but there is one final thing you can do to make sure just in case I am wrong. Just in case The Universe is communicating to you right now by throwing obstacles in your way when you try to pursue your inspirations in life, here's what you can do...... ask The Universe to stop communicating with you in that way.

If up until this point in your life The Universe has been trying to nudge you in the right direction by inspiring you to do something when it wanted you to go in a certain direction and by throwing obstacles in your way when it didn't want you to go in a certain direction, ask it to stop communicating with you in that way.

Instead, ask The Universe to speak to you internally. Ask it to make you feel inspired and alive when you are in alignment with it and your purpose in life, and to make you feel uninspired when you're not. Ask for it and then turn inwards and listen.

Essentially, make an agreement with The Universe to no longer throw obstacles in your way when you're not listening to your intuition. Ask it instead to speak to you internally through your inspirations and your intuitive feelings.

In this way, when you are inspired and excited about manifesting something, and you begin to go after it, if any obstacles come up you'll know that those are all just limiting beliefs manifesting themselves in your life and you'll find a way to overcome them. You'll never have to worry about trying to interpret every obstacle as some kind of sign from The Universe that maybe you shouldn't be doing something.

Remember, when The Universe wants or doesn't want you to do something because it could be disastrous, such as for example the stories I shared previously about being guided to switch lanes while driving to avoid a car accident - the desire to change lanes came to me from <u>an internal source,</u> an intuitive gut feeling screaming at me to get into the left lane. According to the outside world I should have been in the right lane as the outside world was giving me a green light to be in the right lane. It was an **internal** signal from The Universe that inspired me to get into the left lane and avoid a potentially deadly accident.

Keep that in mind. Tune in and listen to your intuition because that is how The Universe speaks to you.

CHAPTER 11 - CONCLUSION

In this book I have shared with the nine main strategies you can utilize to metaphorically take your foot off the brake and press the gas pedal to turbocharge the speed at which you see results with The Law of Attraction.

In the second chapter we discussed the importance of not trying to hack reality. Trying to break the very fabric of your reality by trying to manifest "impossible" things with The Law of Attraction is one of those things that slows down your progress and metaphorically hits the brake.

In chapter three we talked about how your limiting beliefs act as either speed bumps or brick walls in achieving what you desire. We talked about how you can use affirmations or the PSYCH-K® process to get rid of limiting beliefs. This further disengages your brakes.

In chapter four we discussed how destiny and free will play a part in shaping our lives. Understanding that we are all part of The Universe and that our desires are also the desires of The Universe helps us to start pushing the gas pedal.

In chapter five we talked about how we can't understand The Universe with linear thinking. The way that The Universe orchestrates and manifests the things that we desire through the Law of Attraction is a non-linear process. Understanding this helps us to follow our intuition which once again helps us to push the gas pedal even further.

In chapter six we covered the topic of inspired action and how it is different from just taking massive action. By applying inspired action we once again significantly improve our ability to consciously use the Law of Attraction to manifest our desires. With inspired action we push the gas pedal even further.

In chapter seven we talked about the importance of charging up our energy and the importance meaning plays in our lives. By applying meaning to our desires and visualizing them, it is as if we are even further stepping on the gas pedal.

In chapter eight we discussed the topic of selfishness. Getting clear on the fact that the most selfless thing we can do is to "selfishly" act in accordance with our inspired desires eliminates the guilt many of us feel when trying to manifest greatness in our lives. This metaphorically takes our foot further off the brake.

In chapter nine we talked about the importance of understanding and accepting the role that intention energy plays in our lives, and not to dismiss this energy just because it is invisible to us. With the full power of intention behind us, we are now fully ready to hit the gas pedal full throttle.

And finally in chapter ten we talked about how The Universe communicates with us through our internal intuition, and not by throwing obstacles in our way. We also learned that it is not the obstacles or challenges themselves which slow us down, but our mistaken belief that maybe these obstacles are signs from The Universe.

By realizing that it wouldn't make any sense for The Universe to first inspire us to want something and then to try to prevent us from having it, we can eliminate any doubt that anything we are inspired to want in our lives is also in alignment with The Universe.

This final realization, will hopefully help us to fully release the brakes, taking us on a turbocharged journey towards achieving the lives of our dreams.

I hope you enjoyed this book, and thank you for taking this journey with me. Now take these nine strategies and apply them in your life, and you will see results faster than you have ever seen before!

ABOUT THE AUTHOR

Paul Piotrowski is an entrepreneur, blogger, coach, Internet marketer and a polymath / scanner. He regularly blogs on the topics of personal development, spirituality, health and fitness, Internet marketing and making money online on his blog at www.Paulymath.com.

He lives in Maple Ridge, BC, Canada with his wife Drea, and their two dogs Kobe and Zoe.

Contact:

Website: www.Paulymath.com

Email: paul@paulymath.com

Made in the USA
Charleston, SC
19 February 2011